101 Essays to Empower You to Rise & Thrive

Frank Agin
Founder & President
AmSpirit Business Connections

ISBN: 978-1-967521-02-9

Published by:
418 Press, A Division of Four Eighteen Enterprises LLC
Post Office Box 30724, Columbus, Ohio 43230-0724

In appreciation of
Gina Winterstein

Forever the first
Area Director of

Am*Spirit*

BUSINESS *CONNECTIONS*

Table of Contents

Look For These Other Books in This Series

101 Essays to Empower You to Up Your Game
101 Essays to Empower You to Build Momentum
101 Essays to Empower You to Limitless Reach
101 Essays to Empower You to Elevate Your Influence
101 Essays to Empower You to Peak Performance
101 Essays to Empower You to The Winning Edge
101 Essays to Empower You to Live Unstoppable
101 Essays to Empower You to Achieve Greatness
101 Essays to Empower You to Break Barriers

Introduction

This book comes from the insight and creativity of Frank Agin.

Who is Frank? He is the founder and president of AmSpirit Business Connections, an organization that empowers entrepreneurs, sales representatives, and professionals to become successful and gain more referrals through networking.

He is the author of several books, including *Foundational Networking: Building Know, Like and Trust to Create a Lifetime of Extraordinary Success* and *The Three Reasons You Don't Get Referrals*. See all his books and programs at frankagin.com.

Finally, Frank shares information and insights on professional relationships, business networking and best practices for generating referrals on the Networking Rx podcast.

In the summer of 2018, he started planning this short-form podcast. As he mapped out what he wanted to bring to an audience of entrepreneurs, sales representatives, and professionals, he knew he'd have hundreds of programs.

But in addition to all that content, Frank noticed he also had a plethora of other materials—instructive, insightful, and inspirational. All this additional content was worthwhile, but none of it was long enough to create a full episode of Networking Rx.

Not wanting the material to go to waste, Frank developed it into short essays—approximately 150 words each. Then he started to record and share those segments daily under the brand Networking Rx Minute.

For years, he shared a daily message of empowerment, intuition, and hope. This is a compilation of 101 of those essays. Enjoy.

-1-
Action Breeds Confidence

Do you know what breeds confidence? Do you know what empowers courage? Do you know what builds optimism? It's one simple thing. Action.

You see, setbacks tend to drag down our spirits. Staring at a daunting amount of work can be depressing. Embarking onto or into something new can seem frightening.

However, whenever you take action. No matter how small a step you take you serve to take control of the situation. And this control sets in motion powerful psychological forces that lift your psyche ... it emboldens your consciousness ... it drives you forward.

So, if you're having one of those days, or if you feel like one might be coming your way ... don't shrink from it.

Remember, action breeds confidence. It empowers courage. It builds optimism. So, go out and get busy.

-2-
Prelude to Greatness

Today, here is an assignment. Pick a moment. Stop. And look around.

Do you know what you'll see? You'll see greatness.

Just take a moment and look. You'll see it. If you want.

You'll see people serving their community. You'll see people working hard to provide for themselves and others. You'll see people caring about one another.

Just look. You'll see it.

Ignore what the news might tell you. Displace your notion of what you think greatness should be. Greatness can and should be following through with ordinary lives.

And by this definition, you have every opportunity to be great today. Get out there and work hard at whatever you do. See through your obligations with your family, friends and community.

And these actions will inspire others, because they've stopped to look for greatness too.

Today, is your opportunity. Now, go be great.

-3-
Rehearse, Rehearse, Rehearse

Do you tend to get tongue-tied when meeting someone new or out networking? Are you ever at a loss for words? Have you frozen up when leaving messages or talking on the phone?

There is no shame in any of this. After all, everyone has at one time or another.

But, if you are looking to avoid this, then practice what you have to say. Whether you do it inside your head or talk out loud, there is nothing wrong with rehearsing responses to likely questions or practicing statements you might make in a conversation.

If you get in the habit of taking time to think through what you have to say (or want to say) before you embark on any sort of networking endeavor, you will give a better message. More importantly, however, you will get more respect from the encounter.

-4-
Networking: What is it Really?

What is Networking? Simply helping and being helped by others, and nothing more.

Given that definition, the universe of potential networking is very broad. The universe can include prospecting and selling, but it is much bigger than that. It also includes, servicing clients, volunteering, and even socializing.

In fact, successful networking is something you need to focus on every waking moment. It is and has been part of everything in your life.

It's not just about finding a job, getting clients, or landing a promotion. It can also be about finding a golf league, or that next great vacation. Networking is human interaction and working together so we all can prosper.

Networking is as old as time, and it works. It just takes interacting with others, exploring how you can help them and asking for help in return.

-5-
The Gift of Receiving

You've probably heard the "age old" adage: It's better to give than receive.

You know what? It's true!

By giving and helping others, you brand yourself as someone of value ... people cannot help but know, like and trust you and, you feel a warmth overcome you.

You know what? Others deserve to experience that too. So never be too proud to accept help from another. Don't be that Lone Ranger and try to make it on your own. Be open to encouragement, ideas, and assistance. Let people know what you're looking for.

This is called the Gift of Receiving ... because by opening yourself to the assistance, help and gifts from others, you are giving them the joy of helping you. And from that, they get to feel an incredible warmth overcome them.

So, how could someone help you?

-6-
Anyone Equals No One

What's a good referral for you? Who would you like to meet?

Those are great questions ... and ones I'm sure you long to hear.

The important thing is to be ready with an answer ... and don't have your answer be ANYONE or ANYBODY.

Why? When you say a good referral for me is ANYONE or I'd like to meet ANYBODY, those listening tend to tune it out. It becomes white noise. In short, ANYONE or ANYBODY becomes NO ONE and NOBODY. And you don't want that, right?

Rather, try being as specific as possible. For example, a realtor might say, "A good referral for me is the young couple with a new child. That is the perfect time to find the right house."

When you're this specific, it serves to program the minds of others to subconsciously look for what you've requested.

-7-
When Things Go Wrong

Life is full of challenges. Your health will meet with challenges. Your professional life will meet with challenges. Your relationships will meet with challenges.

In these times, it's easy to get down. It's easy to get frustrated. It's easy to feel as if your whole world is imploding.

To stop that line of thinking, do one or more of the following.

1. Write down the perceived threat and recast it as an opportunity. There is likely a silver lining.

2. Regarding the perceived threat, think through the likely worst-case scenario. Things are probably not as bad as you think, and,

3. Make a list of the things in your life that are going well. Chances are, you have great stuff going on in your life.

While none of these exercises will make your challenges go away, they will offer you a fresh perspective.

-8-
Exchanging Business Cards

Networking is about making contacts and then building those contacts into longstanding, productive relationships. It's a process. One that is very rewarding.

Certainly, an early part of this process is exchanging business cards, right?

When someone offers you a business card, take a lesson from the Far East ... use both hands to receive it. And when you get it, don't just tuck it away. Rather take a few moments to examine it. Perhaps ask for clarification on their name or remark on the logo or tagline or comment on their location.

Why? You see, these little things send a subtle, but vital, message that they are important, and you appreciate your connection to them. And that will help them to come to know, like and trust you ... which is imperative to a long-term relationship.

-9-
No Competition for Excellence

It seems that competition is a part of everyday life and you're competing for everything. But it doesn't have to be.

Here's the reality, you don't need to be better than anyone. You just need to be better than yourself.

That is, everyday strive to be a little better than who you were the day before. Be a little smarter. Make an improvement to your product, your service or how you do your job. Be a little more helpful in serving those around you.

All these improvements add up, moving you closer and closer to being excellent.

And do you know what? There is NO competition for excellence. So, when you get to this point, the competition is chasing you.

-10-
The Game of Change

In 1963, the Mississippi State University men's basketball team aspired to the national championship. Standing in its way, however, was more than just other hopeful teams. No, the biggest obstacle was centuries of racial prejudice.

You see, the Bulldogs needed to confront an unwritten rule stating it was not permitted to play against teams that had "colored" players ... and its first opponent was Loyola University, a team with four African American starters.

Remember, however, the team had big aspirations. So, in the face of requests to forfeit, a looming court injunction from the Governor, and threats of death from the Ku Klux Klan ... the team flew out of state literally under the cloak of darkness to chase its dream.

The lesson. Have BIG Dreams. And don't let anything stand in the way of going after them.

-11-
Three Recurring Themes in Networking

Networking is simply people working together to find mutual benefit. Important to this are three important themes.

First, effective networking involves giving to others first, with no expectation of any return – simply trusting that things will come back to you. As such, you work hard to find ways to help others with referrals, contacts, information, encouragement, and your time.

Second, we do business with people we know, like, and trust. So, everything you do involving others needs to center on you getting to know them, being perceived as likable, and conducting yourself so they feel they can trust you.

And third, remember that everyone you encounter has opportunity. While they might not be your next employer or key business contact, they are somehow connected to someone who might be. Thus, treat them accordingly.

These themes are the foundation upon which all effective relationships are built.

-12-
The Power of One

When you attend social functions, business gatherings or chamber events, the quantity of contacts you make is meaningless. The important thing is the quality of the relationships you develop.

In short, there is an inverse correlation between the number of relationships you attempt to maintain and the quality of those relationships.

So, when you're off to that next networking event, while there may be lots and lots of people, your goal should be to only connect with a handful of them - one by one - in a meaningful way.

This takes the pressure off you to makes lots of new contacts, which is helpful if you do not consider yourself adept at working the room. This also ensures that you put a great effort into getting to know the people with whom you connect, which will enhance your networking results.

-13-
Cultivate Relationships

Although meeting new people is an important part of developing a great network, you can also develop your network by cultivating relationships with people you already know.

Think about it. You already know more people than you will meet over the next year. Therefore, to maximize your networking efforts, rather than devoting the lion's share of your attention to meeting new people, you should also focus on reconnecting with those you already know.

The advantage of reconnecting with these people is that you already have somewhat of a relationship with them.

They know you. They presumably already like you. And they feel a degree of trust towards you.

These elements of networking – know, like and trust – are the building blocks for great things and with those you're already familiar with, that foundation is already built. So why not take advantage of it?

-14-
Interested vs. Interesting

Do you want people to be interested in you? Sure, you do! Who doesn't?

Here's the secret to making it happen: Focus your attention on being interested in them first.

Yes, this sounds counterintuitive, but it's true. As you interact with others, remember that your energy should be focused on being genuinely interested in them.

Learn their name. Find out where they are from. Listen to what they have to say and use it to lead into other questions. Be completely fascinated in who they are, what they do and how they do it.

As strange as it sounds, if you devote yourself to being interested in them, they will come to really like you. They'll find you incredibly interesting. They'll want to know more. And, just like that, you'll have their attention.

-15-
Help Your Network Help You

Know this, you've got a network of people who want to help you. So, ask for help.

But as you do, don't make the mistake of only asking for those opportunities that serve to make your month, quarter, or year. Sure, these would be great, but these are not always easy to come by.

And if this is all you ever ask for, you make it hard for people to help you, which doesn't serve you or them.

So, help your network help you. Don't always ask for the big opportunities. Ask those small ones, too. You know, opportunities that you might not be excited about, but ones that serve to nudge you forward.

Here is the reality: The small things generally lead to bigger things and, more often than not, without the smaller things, the big things never happen.

-16-
Who Do You Know

You know people, right? You know lots of people. There are those on you electronic Rolodex ... the ones from LinkedIn, Facebook and whatever is out there. It's amazing, really.

But here's an even bigger thought ... Who do the people you know, know?

Think about it. Connected to certain people around you is a treasure trove of contacts for you. The potential is immense.

But the potential is not just for you, because as your network expands so does your ability to serve those around you.

So, what are you waiting for? Figure out who you know who is really well connected. Cherish those relationships. Nurture them. Use them to connect you to the rest of the world ... and raise up others in the process.

-17-
The Gift Within Every Adversity

Here's the reality: Bad things happen. Everyone endures setbacks. Accept that.

But here is another reality: While it might seem like these things happen to you, lots of times these things really happen for you. Think about it.

That job loss might really be the impetus for you to start that business you've dreamed about; or ...

The departure of that client you simply cannot afford to lose, actually frees up your schedule so you can find two more just like it; or,

That seemingly horrible break up might well open the door for you to find your one, true soulmate.

Yes, bad things happen, and setbacks are part of life. But when they occur, be sure to take a moment to ponder, "What good might come from this?"

Remember ... Within every adversity look for the gift.

-18-
How Will You Show Up?

When someone comes to you looking for support and assistance, you have three options.

One, you can dismiss it with a disinterested "meh," indicating the issue, whatever it might be, is none of your concern.

Two, you can accommodate them, but approach the task as if it were a chore that inconveniences you.

Or, three, you can enthusiastically show up, with your tone and approach shouting - both figuratively and literally - "What else can I do?"

Which one are you?

Before you answer, ask yourself this: Who do you want showing up for you in your time of need?

Do you want the disinterested disengaged? Do you want the willing, but inconvenienced? Or do you want the enthusiastic contributor to the cause, whatever the "want or need might" be?

So, which are you? Become the person you want in your life.

-19-
Grab The Paper

It turns out your teachers were right. Go figure. Reading is really good for you. It is, however, good for you in ways they never comprehended.

Never underestimate the importance of being better informed. Devote a little time each day to the pastime of reading, whether in print or online. If you focus on a particular sector, peruse a trade journal or two. For added business acumen, get your nose into Inc., BusinessWeek, or a similar periodical.

Not only does the information you glean make you more informed, enlightened and well-rounded, it adds to your personal value. And this is powerful.

You see, the more you know, the more interesting you are and the more you can add to those around you. And the more you have to offer, the more that people will want you in their world. So, read.

-20-
The Proper Networking Mindset

Know this, you've done nothing alone. No one has. We all rely on others to achieve. This is how it's always been. This is how it'll always be. Your relationships with those around you are vital and thus you need to keep these thoughts in mind.

First, believe that relationships are important. With that, you'll be more committed to devoting time and energy to them.

Second, everything you do impacts those relationships. Every action, statement or encounter serves to affect all your relationships.

And third, not every day is going to be a good one. As such, if you are not in the right frame of mind (and cannot get there), spare your relationships, stay home, off the phone, away from e-mail.

Your ultimate success depends on great relationships. Make them a priority.

-21-
Heroic Opportunity Statements

You want to help people. You do. Admit it. It's just who you are.

Here's the problem: Few people come out and ask for help. For example, chances are you don't often hear, "Could you refer me to a good realtor?"

However, what you might hear are statements like, "Man, with a new kid, our house is too small." Or "With the kids off to college, the house is too big." Or "The neighborhood has gotten too noisy."

While these only reference opportunities for realtors, they serve to underscore the point: People are making statements to you every day that contain clues as to the things they need help with.

Listen for those clues, engagement those people in conversation about their pain and then, using your network, find a way to help.

-22-
No One Cares What You Know

You'll hear from time to time that knowledge is power. To a degree that's true. The more you know, the more solid your position in life becomes.

But ultimate power doesn't come from knowledge. Rather it comes from caring.

Here's the reality, no one cares how much you know, until they know how much you care. Ideas, facts and figures pale in comparison to a genuine affection for the well-being of others.

Care for others first. From that, they will want to know you. With that, they will be interested in what you know.

Today, work to enhance your power. Devote time and attention to finding ways to demonstrate your caring for others, personally and professionally. You'll feel your power build as you do.

-23-
Network To Build Your Net Worth

Your life is comprised of various assets. There is physical capital such as money, investments, homes, cars, and other belongings. There is human capital, such as your ability to work, think and do things. And there is social capital, which is the invisible benefit that all your personal and professional relationships provide.

With that in mind, think of your time interacting with others as an important investment. Certainly, some networking offers a better return than others, but it's all an investment.

Prospecting: An investment.
Attending An Event: An investment.
Volunteering: An investment.
Socializing: An investment.

Think about networking as a component of building your personal wealth. When you interact with others, you build value in your life. So, get out and network. As you do, feel as if your net worth is growing, because it is.

-24-
Your 30-Second Commercial

People are going to ask, so you best be ready with an answer.

What are they going to ask? Simply this: What do you do?

This is your moment and you've got 30-seconds - roughly 75 words - to share.

In that time, you need to clearly articulate, who you are, what you do, why it's unique, and how they could help you.

People are going to ask, so be ready. Think about it. Write it out. Review it. Practice it often.

So, what is it that you do? Go!

-25-
Be a Great Day

Do you know what today is? Today is going to be a great day.

If you're listening to this, you've got a roof over your head or a car to drive, access to incredible technology, and the wonder of electricity to power it.

Sure, there are things you still aspire to. And yes, some have more than you. What of it?

For you, here and now, it's going to be a great day. You just need to get out there and figure out what great things await you.

Now, go make it a great day!

-26-
Assessing Your Networking Asset

Networking builds value in your life, know that. How much? That depends on your answer to three basic questions.

Number 1: "Who do you know?" You likely know lots of people, and as you meet more your social capital grows.

Number 2: "Of all the people you know, how many of those people know each other?" You want to have a broad, diverse network where you know lots of people and they are relatively disconnected from one another.

Number 3: "Of the people you know, who do they know that you don't?" You're better off knowing relatively few, but well-connected people than to be connected to a plethora of poorly connected souls.

Think about your answers to these questions. In so doing, you'll assess the value of your network. More importantly, your answers will give you insight as to how you can improve your network value.

-27-
No Shortage of Networking Activities

If you're looking to get connected in today's world there is really no shortage of networking opportunities.

Of course, there are face-to-face opportunities where you are out and about with people interacting in organizations, attending events, or just intermingling over coffee or a round of golf.

But in the modern age, much of what you can do in person, you can now also accomplish via electronic means, such as over the telephone, through an e-mail or via text.

And most recently, innovations have given way to social media applications like LinkedIn, Facebook, Twitter and more. Each allows you to network on a massive scale, on a worldwide basis, 24 hours a day, seven days a week, and all with incredible information about your networking partner even before you make contact.

So, if you're looking to get connected, there is nothing stopping you.

-28-
Handshake Etiquette

Chances are, whenever you encounter someone, you're meet with two things: A smile and a handshake.

Our smiles are innate, natural, almost reflexive.

Handshakes, however, are something we learned somehow along the way.

Wherever and however, you picked up this custom, it's important that you ensure that you have a good handshake.

After all, no one likes a "bone-crushing" handshake. And for that matter, no one appreciates a "limp fish," either.

Focus on striking a balance between the two. Warm. Firm. Thumb-web to thumb-web.

As you work to perfect yours, bear this in mind … It is much better to not be remembered for your handshake, than to be remembered for having a bad one.

-29-
A Lesson from the Heartland

In 2003, the wrestling coach at Kearney High School (near Lincoln, Nebraska) asked senior Brandon Teel to wrestle a freshman from another high school.

This, however, was no ordinary request. You see, Brandon's opponent was a young boy with Down Syndrome.

Brandon's coach asked him to please not hurt his opponent. Just give the freshman the feel of a competitive wrestling match, and then in the third period you can pin him.

Brandon, however, did much more. You see, he got caught up in the atmosphere of cheers for his opponent. Picking the appropriate moment, he allowed himself to be pinned. In so doing, he gave the young freshman a victorious moment of a lifetime.

The lesson is that opportunities to exhibit great compassion do not find you; rather you find them. So, get out and fine one today.

-30-
The Porcupine Fable

Admit it, we long to connect with people just like us and we want to find the people with whom we perfectly agree.

The reality is that no two people are the same and no two people are a perfect complement to one another. It is just a fact of life. Everyone is going to rub us the wrong way at some time or another. What of it?

We ought to take a lesson from the prickly porcupines. They are equipped with thousands of sharp, pointy quills, which serve to protect them from large predators. Yet, they live in cold, cold climates and need to snuggle to share body heat.

Yes, they unintentionally prick and poke their den mates on occasion. But if they didn't huddle, they would surely freeze.

So, people might rub you the wrong way. But you still really need them.

-31-
Not All Giving Is Created Equal

All giving is good, but it doesn't all come from the same spirit. Think about it.

When you give to others …

Do you do so with an air of exasperation under your breath?

Do you do give only because they've asked you?

Do you give only a minimal amount even though you honestly could give more?

Do you give simply to gain the recognition of others?

Do you give out of a sense of obligation?

Or do you give for no other reason than because it's the right thing to do?

While all giving is generous and arguably a wonderful act of kindness, you should know that not all giving is created equal.

Some giving is simply more honorable than others. How noble is your generosity?

-32-
Overcoming Being a Pain

Have you ever hesitated contacting someone because you felt you might be a 'pain in the neck,' or think you might be imposing on them? The answer is likely, yes. We have all had that thought or feeling.

Now, ask yourself this: In contacting someone, "Am I attempting to sell them on something or am I truly trying to add value to them?"

If your genuine motive for making contact is to add value to their life, you should have no reluctance. Anyone would welcome contact that benefits them.

Knowing that, before contacting someone, find that thing (or things) that would truly provide them value. Business referrals? Key Introductions? Important information?

With this value, make the contact. While not every situation will work out, many certainly will (and some in a big way) – those alone will be worth all the effort.

-33-
The Value of An Encouraging Word

What's a youth soccer coach to do? His U9 Gahanna Arsenal team had just been trounced – five zip – in a morning game. As a result, his eight-year-old goalie was left demoralized to the point of tears.

What could the coach do?

Well lots. He got down on a knee next to the boy, put his arm around him and told him not to take it so hard. He explained that the goals scored on him were a team failure and not just his. He also shared pointers on how the young keeper could improve.

And, finally, the coach reminded him that they had other games to play and that the team, coaches and parents believed in him.

With that, when the afternoon game came, the goalie completely forgot the morning debacle.

Look around. There is someone who could use an encouraging word. Take the time to give them a few.

-34-
Be A Great Ancestor

Father time is undefeated. And you won't be on this Earth forever. In time, you'll grow old and sadly pass.

And when you do, your children, and your children's children, and their kids and so on, will have the opportunity to reminisce about your life and the lasting impact you had.

What do you want them to think? What do you want them to say?

In reality, you have control over those memories and that script.

So, feed your family with great memories to cherish. Give them wonderful stories to share. In essence ... be a great ancestor.

-35-
Are You Selling or Networking?

When you interact with others are you selling or networking? Do you know the difference?

Sales is the simple act of taking away someone's pain or providing them pleasure based on the goods or services you have to offer.

Networking is the noble act of taking away someone's pain or providing them pleasure by any means available.

So, are you selling or networking? Know this ... few people like to associate with those who have a singular and primary directive of selling to them.

Conversely, everyone wants to associate with you if they know you are truly interested in helping them ... especially if that help is something outside of what you sell.

And in the end, those that associate with you will want to buy from you.

The simple lesson is this: If you help first, the sales will ultimately come.

-36-
Networking Boomerangs

Your relationships provide you with opportunities, information, support, and energy as well as additional contacts.

How do you improve the flow of these benefits? It's simple. Provide these benefits to others first. Although counterintuitive, "Give First; Get Second" works.

In her book *People Power*, Donna Fisher refers to this as the "Boomerang Effect." Eventually what you inject into your network comes back to you.

Even though you might not expect someone to reciprocate, when you do something for another, they feel an underlying sense of obligation to return the deed. And chances are, they will do something for you in time. This is human nature, and it's a powerfully compelling force.

So, if you're disappointed with what your relationships are providing, examine what you have been contributing to them. Chances are if you toss a "boomerang" or two, you will revitalize the flow of what you get.

-37-
From Small Talk to Networking Success

Let's face it, "small talk" gets a bad rap. It probably harkens back to the continual chiding our mothers did relative to talking with strangers.

While her warnings were intended to protect us as children from those who might prey on our innocence, we are no longer little kids.

We are big boys and girls. We operate in a grown-up world where strangers become good friends, great clients and reliable vendors.

Still, however, "small talk" gets a bad rap. Far too often people see it as idle chitchat that has no productive value in the professional world.

Understand this: your entire life is formed and held firmly together by relationships. And in most every instance, "small talk" had a big part in the creating the relationship.

So, today, go talk to a stranger. Ssshhh! Mom will never know.

-38-
Baby Steps

If you want a strong, productive network that offers you all sorts of benefits, such as referrals, contacts, information and much more, know this: You can do it.

You CAN build a strong, productive network (and reap all the benefits that come with it). You truly can. And you can do it both online and face-to-face in your community.

Know this, however, you just cannot do it overnight. Nor can you do it in a week, a month, or a year. Networking is a process and not an event. Building a strong, productive network takes effort ... and time.

So, commit to doing something every day to develop your network.

Remember, every action you make and every effort you give is a small baby step to getting you the network you ultimately want.

-39-
Support Those Who Support You

Stop for a moment. Stop to think about your accomplishments. Stop to think about your achievements. Stop to think about all the wonderful accolades you've received.

It's likely quite impressive. Kudos. Give yourself a pat on the back. You deserve it.

Now stop to ponder who are the people who were instrumental in helping you achieve all these things. Family? Friends? Co-workers? Colleagues? Maybe people you barely know?

The reality is that you achieve nothing alone. No one does. We're all surrounded by a network of supporters that help get us over, around and through life's challenges.

You know what? These are the people whom we need to support in return. After all, if you don't support the people who support you, one day you'll have no help you.

And with no support, there will be no achievement. Remember, you achieve nothing alone.

-40-
Your Greatest Day Is Yet to Come

What is the expectation you have for yourself? What do you envision as the result of your determination and hard work? What do you see as the crowning achievement of your life?

Wherever your goals and aspirations have you pointed, you need to develop the mindset or expectation that your greatest day is yet to come. That is, you always need to be looking for more achievement.

This is a simple belief that no matter where you are in life – whether struggling to finally get your degree or looking to step up one more rung on the corporate ladder – that a better day awaits you.

Continually envisioning this day keeps you motivated and striving for more. But more importantly, this powerful attitude attracts people to want to associate with you, because your greatest day is yet to come.

-41-
Start With a Positive

There is no moment in your life that is completely independent of any other point in time. For example, how you did in high school has an impact of where you go to college. Or how you performed on a job assignment will impact what your next assignment will be.

So as each instant is connected to the next, how you conduct yourself in each moment impacts future moments.

And while you can do nothing about the past, you can impact any day from the very beginning.

So, starting today ... start every day with a positive thought, a positive statement, and a positive action. Those simple things will then ripple and build throughout your entire day.

Today! Today is going to be a great day. Can't you just feel it?

-42-
Common Acts of Kindness

Networking is about building relationships and an important aspect of building relationships is giving to and helping others.

Giving and helping others, however, is not limited by what you can offer through your personal wealth, professional experience or influence.

Giving and helping others can and should be about the little things you can share with the world around you. Like,

Parking a little further from the door so others can have the good spots; or,

Stopping and waiting to hold the door for others; or,

Being pleasant with and smiling at everyone you encounter.

This list could go on and on. In fact, there is an almost endless litany of practically unnoticeable niceties that you can do for others.

If you want great relationships in your life, start by making not just random acts of kindness but rather common acts of kindness.

-43-
The Case for Volunteerism

Business, career and even life is tough. Every day is a challenge to hang onto what you have.

If you want to get the upper hand on all of this, there is a simple solution: Volunteer.

Now, you might respond, "Volunteer? I am not looking for another distraction or drain on my limited time."

While this is an understandable response, think about it.

For starters, through volunteering you have the opportunity to build your talents, skills and experiences.

Plus, through volunteering you'll expand your network by working with a diverse corps of individuals who share your passion.

And, finally, study after study shows that people who volunteer are happier, healthier, and live longer lives.

So, if you want a better existence, volunteer. Volunteering – at any level, for any organization – is an activity where you can contribute to others while at the same time benefit yourself.

-44-
Every Contact Has Opportunity

If you're honest with yourself, you have been guilty at one time or another of disregarding someone as not being of consequence to you.

The administrative staffer.
The attendant at the gas station.
The person delivering the newspaper.

Admit it. Everyone's done this. It's easy to do, as these people will not get you that next job, client, or pay raise.

While it is true that not everyone has the potential to be your new employer or next great client, it is also true that everyone knows someone that could. Every contact has opportunity.

This is not to suggest that you need to invite the paperboy to your holiday party or over for the big game.

However, you need to treat everyone with the same attention and respect as you would a new employer or great client – because everyone is connected to one of those people.

-45-
A Pitchless Win

In 2009, Colorado Rockies pitcher Alan Embree was credited with the win in a game against the Washington Nationals. Nothing monumental, right?

What was monumental, however, was that Embree did not throw a pitch - not one - when most pitchers might need over 120 pitches to earn the same achievement.

Nevertheless, through a technical quirk in how baseball statistics are awarded, he was credited with the win without throwing a ball.

Life can be like that. Some of your achievements are a hard-fought grind. And yet others come much, much easier.

Here's the lesson: Whether difficult or easy-peasy, remember all your achievements are earned. Celebrate them.

-46-
You Only Get Thirty

When someone asks what you do, you should be ready with a succinct, well-thought-out response. This introduction – which is an explanation of who you are and what you do – should take no more than 30 seconds.

It, however, should include a short statement establishing your reliability, trustworthiness, and integrity.

What is it about you, your product or service, or the business for which you work that would give someone comfort in wanting to either refer you clients or do business with you directly?

Some examples of this credibility statements are:

"I have been doing this over 25 years and have been involved in business my entire adult life."

"Last year alone, I worked with over 100 clients."

"I use a unique approach that helps me direct clients to the best option."

Whatever works for you, however, needs to be part of your introduction.

-47-
Working The Networking Floor

Networking for career and business is fraught with many challenges.

One can be finding events to attend and network at.

Another might be fitting those events into a busy schedule.

And, then once you've conquered those two challenges, you might be faced with the dilemma of connecting with the right people, especially when there are dozens and dozens of people already in conversation.

To overcome this challenge, take some advice on "working the networking floor" from Andrew Chiodo, a personal branding and public relations expert and author of *The Fine Art of Networking*:

Try positioning yourself in the neighborhood of a person you want to meet. Once you establish eye contact, you have a chance to introduce yourself. Do so quickly, offer a card and ask for one in return.

Give it a try. You'll find that it is quite effective.

-48-
The Best Way to Get Referrals

Are you looking for referrals? Great. The best way to get them is simply this: Give referrals first.

You see, as humans, we are hardwired to help the people who are helping us. Thus, when you give referrals, the people on the receiving end feel a great sense of commitment to you. Even those who watch you give referrals to others develop a sense of loyalty to you (as you are serving to contribute to others).

Of course, this is in no way a guarantee. And you should never give with an expectation. Rather give to others and follow that with a heavy dose of patience (as depending on the situation, the giving-to-getting cycle can take time).

So, if you truly want to generate more referrals for yourself in the future, start by hunting down referrals for others today.

-49-
Stone Soup for the Network

The fable *Stone Soup* is the tale of a peddler's efforts to inspire famished villagers to share food amongst each other by ceremoniously placing an ordinary stone into a boiling cauldron of water.

As the brew simmers, he pledges to share with all as he coaxes and entices onlookers to make "their" soup even better by contributing carrots, cabbage, and beef.

This a wonderful metaphor for how simple acts of generosity can inspire a network to become productive.

At first, people in a network holdback, hesitant to contribute. Then one day someone does something. Makes an introduction. Shares information. Refers business.

This simple act becomes contagious. It leads to another and another. Then those small acts start to grow in stature. Soon, everyone is involved in a frenzy of networking – all this from one small act.

What could you do today to spark something similar?

-50-
Networking Yields Positive Results

Henry Ford is credited with saying: "Whether you think you can, or you think you can't, you're right."

Ford's point was simply: Your beliefs are powerful things, and they often drive the end result.

This same logic applies to networking success. If you believe that networking yields positive results, then it will lead to positive results. It you don't believe that networking does anything for you, then ... well, you know.

If you're on the fence between these two extremes, however, here's a way to get you believing.

Write down one time where someone did something for you. A referral. An introduction. Shared useful information. Got it? There you go. Networking worked. Now think of another. Write it down. Keep thinking and jotting.

As your list grows so will your belief that networking is a powerful force in your life.

-51-
Waiting On Reciprocity

The best way to get from your network is to give to it first.

When can you expect things to come back to you?

Well, you can't. Sometimes it's immediate. Other times you wait days, weeks, months, and still other times it can be years.

Consider this … in 1990, after Mexico City suffered a disastrous earthquake, the government of Mexico received a $5,000 contribution from Ethiopia … who at the time was ravaged by famine.

Daily, its people were literally dying by the hundreds. Why would Ethiopia not keep the money for use with its own people?

The Ethiopian Relief Agency responded, "In 1935, when Italy invaded, Mexico *helped* us."

This simply serves as confirmation that if we give and trust, eventually opportunities, information, support, energy, and additional contacts will come back to you.

-52-
A Case for Business Cards

Imagine this: You've walked into a meeting you're slated to be at. And there with you is that local business icon you've been hoping to meet. Then it happens. You and icon are face to face. Shaking hands. Going through the polite pleasantries.

Then, the meeting is called to order and the icon says, "Please give me your card ... I'd love to continue this over coffee."

You grab for your cards and realize that you only have one. And it looks like you've had it tucked away for ages. Smudged. Slightly torn. And definitely dog-eared.

Not ideal, huh?

Make sure you always have on you clean, crisp business cards. And, just in case, be sure you have an emergency stash in your car.

You only have one chance to make a first impression. Don't blow it with a bad business card.

-53-
Accomplished Because You're Connected

Think about your life. Take an inventory of all your accomplishments, personal and professional. Make an accounting of all the milestones you've attained.

No doubt, the litany of achievements is impressive. You might not think so at first blush … but give yourself some credit. You've got an accomplished life. And, likely, you're aspiring for more.

All of this didn't just happen, right? There was lots of hard work, for sure. And, yes, you were strategic. But there were also lots of people along the way helping, encouraging, and supporting you.

In reality, you're accomplished because you're connected. It's the network around you empowering that success … giving you referrals … introducing you to key contacts … and sharing vital information.

So, if you want to be more accomplished, work on being more connected to those you know and those you're to meet.

-54-
Always Room for Improvement

A corporate trainer asks the class, "What's the biggest room at your office?"

The attendees fire out answers, naming a litany of possibilities. For each the trainer responds "NO."

When the attendees have seemed to exhaust the possibilities, the trainer shares. "The biggest room at your office is the room for improvement."

While the question is sort of a ruse, the answer is spot on. No matter where you are professionally - no matter how much you've achieved, no matter what - you have room to improve and should continually act upon it.

Read. Listen to podcasts. Attend seminars. Keep up on your industry or profession. Listen to and learn from colleagues, vendors and, even, competitors.

Take any and every opportunity to improve yourself, which serves to allow you to add value to those around you.

-55-
Prompt Action

From time-to-time people impair the flow of opportunities they get from their networks by not taking reasonably immediate action when someone refers them business or offers them a contact or points them towards useful information.

Think about it: Doing nothing sends the message they you aren't interested in the help they're offering. With that, they stop offering, and of course, you don't want that.

No doubt, life can be busy. And sometimes you become consumed with too much business. Know this (if you don't already), business cycles. If you are not careful, a full plate can become empty before you know it.

The lesson is simple. When someone offers you a referral, introduces you to a new contact or gives you a tip on useful information, get after it. Demonstrate that you value the opportunity with prompt action.

-56-
Asking For Help

Know this. people want to help you – they really do. It's human nature.

No, they aren't looking to put your entire life on their shoulders and not rest until you're a booming success. But they do want to help you, personally and professionally.

They'd be happy to refer you some business. They'd be willing to introduce you to a key contact. They'd be delighted to share information on that awesome weekend getaway.

What stopping them? Simple: You not asking.

So, if you're helpful to your network, then feel free to ask of it, too. In life, no one gets to succeed alone. What kind of help do you need? Make a list. Then brainstorm who might be someone good to ask. Finally, pick up the phone, work up an e-mail or arrange for coffee.

Whatever it is, however, you do it, ask for help.

-57-
360 Degree Networking

Often, when people think of networking, they think of it in terms of using it to achieve professional goals, being referred to clients or making a career move. That's true. Networking is this ... this and so much more.

Networking, which is nothing more than building relationships with those around you, is a valuable means of support and achievement for all areas of your life, including finances, health, social, recreation, hobbies, and even vacation.

Your life is built upon and held together by relationships, which is networking. So, it only makes sense to apply sound networking skills to all areas of your life.

Not only will that provide you with greater all-around success, but the additional practice will serve to make you better at professional networking.

-58-
Team Chemistry

In a 2002 edition of the *Academy of Management Journal*, three researchers presented their finding on a study involving the National Basketball Association.

In the study, they clearly illustrated that teams who routinely altered their player rosters performed much worse than teams who kept the roster somewhat consistent. This probably comes as no surprise, right?

However, this might be a surprising thought. Your network is in essence a team. And like the NBA, it performs best when the so-called roster remains intact and learns to gel.

No, the relationships in your network aren't perfect. None ever are. Over time, however, the people in your network learn about you and you learn about them. From that, the relationship becomes productive and that's most important. And this will only get better in time.

So, if you want a championship business, profession, or life, keep your team intact.

-59-
An Awesome Kick

Anna Powell was a member of the Ridgewood High School girls' soccer team. There, she wasn't all-state, all-conference, or even the team's all-star. She wasn't the player that her teammates depended on to score that winning goal or save that final shot.

One thing her teammates did depend on her for though, was a powerful kick. Through much practice she attained a powerful kick. An awesome kick that even led to some far-off goals.

In fact, her kick was so powerful, so awesome that she didn't limit herself to soccer. You see, when the football team's kicker was lost to an injury, they enlisted Anna and her awesome kick to lead them in the state playoffs.

Like Anna, you've worked hard, and you've honed many wonderful talents. Don't limit yourself. Rather, use your talents wherever you can add value.

-60-
A Feel-Good Habit

If you're looking for an easy and yet highly effective means of cultivating goodwill amongst all the relationships in your life - personal and professional - start by saying "Thank You."

Those two words (or some form of them) do wonders to lift the spirits of those you impart them on. And in return, these people appreciate you for acknowledging them, which feels good for you too.

Here's the thing: There is no shortage of reasons to thank others. You can thank people for anything. You can thank people for everything. You can even say thank you for people telling you thank you.

Saying thank you is also a great way to build relationships. Saying thank you should become a habit. Not just a good habit, though, but one that makes you feel good too.

Oh, by the way, thanks for listening!

-61-
The Unpredictable Nature of Networking

Relationship building or networking works! But by its very nature, the results are unpredictable.

Networking works, but it may not work HOW you would like it to work. For example, you go to a networking event hoping to build a clientele. To that end, nothing pans out, but there you learn of a great vacation opportunity. Networking worked.

Networking may not work WHERE you want it to work. The next day standing in line to get coffee, you strike up a conversation with someone who reveals in polite chit-chat that they are looking to be a client for someone like you.

Finally, networking may not work WHEN you expect it to. That event seems to yield no clients. Then after a month, a year, or even more, someone reconnects and signs on.

Networking works. You just can't predict how, where or when it will.

-62-
Diagram It!

If you're looking for a useful exercise to help your networking become more effective, take the time to create a visual representation of your network.

This can be as simple as starting with a single sheet of paper and a pencil. From there, write your name in the middle and then draw lines representing the major branches of your network, such as family/friends, business, community relations and volunteer connections.

At the end of each spoke, jot down the names of the key individuals associated with each branch. Then draw lines between individuals on different branches indicating who knows whom.

No, this isn't a perfect representation of your network. But this will provide you with a greater awareness of the resources you have available to you. And it will give you a better sense as to how you can add value to those you know. Give it a try.

-63-
Small Talk Creates Networking Bonds

When it comes to networking, small talk is big.

You see, it's through "small talk" that people gain an understanding of who you are, what interests you, how you spend your time. And you learn the same about them.

As an analogy, "small talk" is like the warmup you do before you really get into the work out.

It is the foundation of the KNOWING in "Know, Like & Trust". It is also this small foundation upon which people gain a sense as to whether they LIKE you.

In fact, social science and brain studies have shown that in the few minutes where chitchat is happening, people even start to formulate a sense as to whether they can TRUST you.

So, when you encounter an opportunity to engage in small talk, don't shy away. Embrace it.

-64-
Networking As a House

When it comes to a house, there is always something in need of repair.

Furnaces falter and need to be fixed. Door hinges squeak and must be oiled. And even the best paint jobs don't last forever.

The same is true of the relationships that make up your network. They require maintenance too, as they are not immune to neglect and decay.

For example, you and a client may seem out of sync. You can fix it with time on the phone.

Your interaction with a colleague may seem rusty. You can oil it up over a warm cup of coffee.

Even though a friendship may seem to be humming along, an encouraging e-mail will help to keep it that way.

Your network will always need a degree of maintenance. Know that. Accept that. And just like a house, keep a list of what you need to work on next.

-65-
Believe In Networking

Do you know the most important thing for successful networking? Guess!

A solid 30-second commercial? No! That's not even close.

Going to lots of events and activities? Spending time on LinkedIn and other social media? Knowing lots of people? Nah, no and nope!

Volunteering in your community? No, but that's a great thought.

Finding ways to add value to people you know? That's important, but not the most important.

Give up? Okay, the most important thing for successful networking is first believing. Believing that networking is a worthwhile endeavor. Believing that networking works.

If you don't believe in networking, then nothing you do will matter. This lack of confidence will come through in your demeanor and your results will be disappointing, at best.

If, however, you believe that networking will yield positive results, then that's exactly what you'll get.

-66-
Building Trust

You're trustworthy. At least, that's what you aspire to, right? In short, you simply want others to trust you.

Here's the secret; if you want people to trust you, you simply need to trust them first.

Think about it: If someone coldly remarks, "I don't trust you" what's your reaction? You're taken back. Your posture becomes tense. You think, "if that's what they think of me, it'd be risky to trust them." So, you don't.

But if someone remarks, "I trust you," your reaction is completely different. You relax. A warm feeling comes over you. You can't help but smile and feel good about them. From that, trust naturally ensues.

The lesson is simple. Trust people. This is not to suggest taking senseless risks. But there are lots of sensible ways you can trust others and let them know it too.

-67-
Be a Networking Sleuth

Dale Carnegie once remarked, "You can make more friends in two months by becoming really *interested* in other people than you can in two years by trying to be *interesting* to other people."

Nevertheless, far too often people get this backwards. They want to stand out, seem remarkable, be downright impressive. So, they share, share, share and put the best possible spin on everything.

And as they do, they miss a wonderful opportunity to endear themselves to others by discovering what makes THEM stand out, how they're remarkable and impressive.

Don't make this mistake. Be interested in others. Become a networking sleuth and each and every day make it your mission to find something new about someone you know. If you do this, not only will you uncover something wonderful, but people will really appreciate you for making the effort.

-68-
Life Is a Decathlon

C.K. Yang entered the 1960 Olympic Games with aspiration of becoming a gold medalist in the decathlon, a grueling two-day, 10-event competition.

Yang was the favorite to win. After all, he had already won the 1954 and 1958 Asian Games. Yang had both the training and confidence to become the Olympic champion.

Unfortunately, things didn't work out for him. In the end, he only did well enough to earn the silver. Although he had the best performance in seven of the ten decathlon events, in three events he scored relatively poorly.

At the same time, American Rafer Johnson had done consistently well in all ten decathlon events. This earned him the gold medal and title of "the world's greatest athlete."

The lesson is that success in life is not about doing a few things great. Rather, success in life is about doing consistently well at everything.

-69-
Your Network's MVP

Who is the most valuable person in your network?

After all, not all your contacts are the same. Some are simply outstanding, and others, well, not so much. And the vast majority are somewhere in between. But one is the very, very best.

Do you know who it is? The simple answer is that the most valuable person in your network is [drumroll, please], YOU! Think about it.

No one cares about you more than you do. No one is more reliable towards you than you. And no one is in a better position to deliver your hopes, dreams, and aspirations.

There is no question that your network consists of various contacts. Some are good, some are bad and there are those that lie in between. But when it comes to who has the most ability to carry you to greatest heights, it is, no doubt, you. So today, be sure to take care of your MVP.

-70-
Business Card Branding

While your business card will not build your network, per se, it does impact how your network perceives you. Believe that.

As such, you should ensure that your business card reflects your professional image. You should never skimp on the design or production of this marketing piece ... yes, marketing piece. Enlist a professional to help with the layout and design. Pay careful attention to colors. Use quality cardstock.

In fact, your business card should be considered an integral part of your entire brand strategy. Take every step to ensure that your business cards follow the same graphics standards as the rest of your communications materials, such as letterhead, brochures, and even your website.

Your business card is more than just a first impression. It has the power to have a dynamic lingering effect on those who see it. Invest in it.

-71-
In Sight; Top of Mind

The mantra of love may well be that "Absence makes the heart grow fonder" but that does not apply to networking. Rather, with networking the refrain no doubt is, "Out of sight; out of mind."

Simply put, consistent interaction with your connections is critical.

Sure, everyone gets super busy from time to time. And there are times when you're just not around. But outside of those exceptions, periodic contact is vital to people knowing, liking, and trusting you.

The people in your network are the gateway to many important things, such as business referrals, useful information, and great new contacts. And when you're on their mind, the chances of you getting these things goes way up.

So, if you want the very best from those around you, be in sight and be in contact to ensure you're top of mind.

-72-
It's More Than Who You Know

The saying goes that "It's Not What You Know, But Who You Know." And to a degree that's true.

Despite this, there are many who seemingly know lots of people but gain very little from their network. How is this possible?

The answer is quite simple: You see, effective networking is more than just "who" you know, as success won't come from filling your database with the names of thousands.

Rather, effective networking is about building meaningful relationships.

That is, make every effort to get to know people and at the same time let them know you. In addition, consistently conduct yourself in a pleasant and likable fashion. And, finally, build trust by never wavering from being both honest and reliable.

In summary, effective networking is about more than who you know, it's about how you interact with others.

-73-
Great Scott!

In the summer of 2008, Jericho Scott was just an average nine-year-old growing up in New Haven, Connecticut.

The only problem was that this average boy was a great Little League baseball player. He was so great, in fact, that the parents of opposing teams wanted to ban him from the league. Jericho, however, would not let that stop him.

Life can be like that. As you dream, you'll encounter those who will be naysayers. As you work hard to achieve, there will be others who will try to distract and detract. As you accomplish, there will be some who will attempt to discredit or disqualify you from getting more.

While much of the world will cheer every step of your ascent, there will be some who hope to slow your rise. That's life. After all, mediocrity has always railed against greatness. Endeavor to be great anyway.

-74-
Being An Everyday Hero

Be a hero! You don't have to don a mask or cape. You don't have to do something with lasting historical significance. You don't even need to be a first-responder type.

Nevertheless, be a hero. Be one in an everyday sense where you do something positive that you're not obligated to do.

An everyday heroic feat could certainly be referring someone a new client or providing someone the name of a good mechanic or an honest attorney. It could even be sharing a personal insight or an old family recipe.

Being an everyday hero is simply watching, listening, and thinking "How could I make someone's life a little better." Then when you spot something, swing into action.

From here, not only will your network flourish, but your network will seek to mimic your heroics. That, in time, will benefit you.

So, go be a hero.

-75-
Your Introduction

What do you do? That's an important question and whether you call it an "elevator pitch," "30-second commercial" or whatever, when someone asks, you need to be ready with a response that is clear and concise.

To ensure you're ready at that important moment, use this four-part preparation plan:

First, think through the most significant information to communicate, such as what you do and what makes you unique.

Second, write it out or type it up. This is not to read it. This solidifies the content in your mind.

Next, from time to time, when you have spare moments, review what you've documented. This further etches the message in your mind.

Finally, when you're given the opportunity, don't shrink from the moment. Use the message you've created.

After all, these moments happen without notice, so be ready.

Like now. What do you do? Go!

-76-
The Wonderful Thing About "Thank You"

Beyond just being the right thing to do, saying "thank you" is a power means of helping your networking.

First, networking is about establishing and strengthening relationships. Thus, taking the time to appropriately say "thanks" fortifies those connections in three ways.

First, saying "thanks" serves to further etch you in the minds of those helping you.

Second, saying "thanks" confirms to those helping you that they are doing something of benefit. Knowing they're on the right track makes it likely they'll do more.

Finally, saying "thanks" gives those helping you an uplifting good feeling. And that feeling subconsciously drives them to repeat the behavior, which benefits you.

So, saying "thanks" is more than just the right thing to do, it's also a great way to build the relationships that hold together your network.

And, of course, thank you very much for listening.

-77-
The Networking Sandwich

A good relationship is like a sandwich. The meat is the periodic face-to-face interaction within your network. And the time before and after that interface is the bread.

Believe it or not, it's this bread that is vital to the overall success of networking.

You see, in-person interaction tends to be second nature. They're there with you. You're there with them. Questions, answers, and communication tends to flow. In short, it's easy.

It's, however, the time before and after these face-to-face interactions where your network can suffer. They're out of sight and to a degree out of mind. The relationship can feel as if it's in a state of decay.

Knowing this, if a relationship is important, be sure to devote energy to connecting when you're not together. Phone calls. E-mails. Texts.

Don't just rely on the meat. Also focus on the bread.

-78-
Three Great Networking Questions

Engaging in small talk is a natural part of developing solid, long-term relationships. And the secret to good small talk is getting the other person to share about themselves and then you add commentary from there.

To get the other person talking, you need to arm yourself with a handful of open-ended questions you can use to inspire great conversation.

In his best-selling book *Endless Referrals*, author, speaker and business relationship guru Bob Burg provides "Ten Networking Questions That Work Every Time."

Here are three you can easily add to your arsenal and deploy in your next small talk conversation:

One ... How did you get your start in your business?
Two ... What do you enjoy most about your profession?
Three ... What ways have you found to be the most effective for promoting your business?

Try one or more. Good luck!

-79-
Fourth and 15 Years

In 1982, the Beloit College Buccaneers were trying to break a streak of 15 losing football seasons. The prospects of this didn't look good, however. It was the last game of the season, the team had a 4-and-4 record, and they were down by 28 points halfway through the third quarter.

At this point, the Buccaneer faithful had lost all hope. The players, however, had not.

With just 4:40 left in the third quarter, they scored a touchdown. From this spark, riding a burning desire to succeed, an incredible belief in themselves and a little bit of luck, they scored 33 unanswered points. In so doing, they capped a historic comeback to create a winning season.

Remember this. Wherever you find yourself in life, know that it's never too late and you are never too far down to mount a comeback.

-80-
The Want of More

Here's a stone cold, hardcore fact: Everyone wants to achieve more in life than they currently have. You want to achieve more, right? The wealthiest people on the planet, well, they want to achieve more too. And even the most die-hard couch potato wants something - even if it's only wanting a better couch upon which to "veg."

Everyone wants to achieve more. So, don't wonder if someone could use your help. They could, as they want more. And they would appreciate whatever you do.

Rather than asking "if" you can help, focus your attention on "how" you can help others. Who can you refer them to? What information would serve to benefit them? How can you connect them to opportunities?

Then, take action. This initiative will amaze people. Moreover, it will inspire others to do the same.

-81-
Reflect On

From time to time, getting out and networking can seem like a daunting task. After all, you thrust yourself outside of your comfort zone, sometimes in strange situations, and attempt to reconnect with long-lost contacts and meet new people you know little about.

In these times, self-doubt can seep into your confidence. You doubt your ability to carry a conversation. You question what you have to offer. You question the whole notion of building relationships. You wonder if there might be a higher and better use of your time.

At these moments, to pull you out of this funk, you should reflect on those times when you've been successful through networking. Recall the times that connecting with strangers and old contacts has been worthwhile. These recollections will spur you on and give you the courage you need to face the next great networking experience.

-82-
Creating Solid Networking Relationships

You create solid relationships with people in your life when you set about to make three things happen.

First, you allow people to get to know you and you get to know them.

Second, you conduct yourself so that the people you know come to like you.

And, finally, you operate in a manner that is both honest and reliable, allowing those who know and like you to also trust you.

It's a simple reality: These three things are a powerful component of human nature. As such, people associate with and do business with those they know, like and trust.

So, focus on building these things into your relationships. If you do, then the people around you will be more likely to help you, refer you clients, introduce you to centers of influence, and direct you towards beneficial opportunities.

-83-
Build Credibility

As you meet new people, they certainly want to know who you are and what you do. But they also want to have a sense as to what makes you or your business and what it offers both reliable and trustworthy.

Face it. You aren't the only person who does what you do. And, even if you are, people might be able to live without what you have to offer.

So, it's important to work into your introduction a few words establishing credibility. Brief statements like …

"I have the highest professional designation our industry offers." OR

"Our team has over 60 years combined experience serving clients." OR

"We've found that our product has a 97% satisfaction rating."

These small declarations serve to establish a level of dependability, making it more likely that someone will associate with you, retain your services, or refer you to someone else.

-84-
Vital Networking Attitudes

When you look to improve your networking, where does your mind go? Does it center immediately on tangible things? Are you plotting and scheming to meet more people? Are you crafting that perfect elevator pitch? Are you envisioning having great small talk conversations?

If you are, great. All these skills are important to sound networking. But while these are important, they alone won't create networking success.

What will, however, are three attitudes:

One. Ensure that your outward impression projects a positive, optimistic, and uplifting spirit.

Two. Ensure that your heart is focused on giving and adding value to the world around you.

And three. Ensure that you are intent on conducting yourself with an unwavering degree of honesty and reliability.

Yes, networking skills are important. But what's vital is having the appropriate mindset relative to your presence, your altruism, and your integrity.

-85-
Working Through Tough Times

One of the many great sayings of renowned author and speaker John C. Maxwell is, "When you're winning nothing hurts; when you're losing everything hurts."

It's true, right? When things are working in your favor - you close on a big sale, you get that promotion, or you're picked to take the plum assignment - little bothers you.

But when things are trending against you - you lose a client, you suffer through a sub-par performance review, or, worse yet, you lose your job altogether - every little thing bothers you.

While you cannot control the downs of life, you can control the aftermath. When the sledding gets tough - and it will - figure out what you need to do to work through, over or around the pain or heartache. Then attack that thing. Get yourself back into winning.

-86-
Get Up Out of Your Chair

It is easy to do. You get held up in your office or other workplace, busily doing whatever. You know, pushing paper, organizing e-mails, chatting on the phone, tinkering in social media. Whatever the case, none of it is vital or even important in the short term, but it's there and it's easy to get caught up in.

Well, stop. Don't do the easy thing. The easy thing seldom yields many results. Rather, get yourself up and out. Go be amongst people. Invite someone to coffee. It could be a client, a colleague, or even a vendor.

Although you may consider none of this as true networking, the action will propel you out amongst people. This alone will create a powerful change to your mindset, and as you will be amongst other people that change will lead to networking.

-87-
Serve Others; Lift Yourself

Jeff Olson, head football coach for Michigan's Ishpeming High School, seemingly suffered tragedy after tragedy leading up to the 2012 season, as he endured the unrelated deaths of three young men associated with his program ... one being his own son.

Despite this sorrow, he rallied support so that a senior with Down Syndrome could not only play football but also be his kicker. Coach Olson stuck with that decision even though the senior missed his first six extra points. For this selflessness, karma shined on Olson and his team, as they won the state title.

Everyone faces heartache. In these moments, it's easy to become withdrawn and self-centered. Fight these tendencies, however. Contribute to those around you. Through kind words and selfless actions, life has a wonderful way of balancing itself.

-88-
Table Networking

This can happen: You've become savvy at working a room. Then you show up to a networking function only to find the protocol calls for everyone to sit at tables.

Now what? Your usual tactics and strategies for moving about, mingling, and chatting with others have been completely frustrated.

Don't despair. While you might not be mobile, the same networking etiquette still applies.

In this situation, your first move is to find a table of people with whom you can interact. From there, quietly sit, listen and learn what you can from your table mates. Then at the appropriate moment, start into the conversation by asking questions to draw out others and do what you can to encouraging dialogue among people.

This will brand you as both interesting and a productive facilitator. Plus, it will create a productive experience for you.

-89-
Help Wanted

Life is full of possibilities, isn't it? Or at least that's what we'd like to believe. You tell yourself, "Anything I truly put my mind to, I can achieve." Right? And it's probably true.

There are, however, impossibilities. It's impossible to alter physical laws, like gravity. It's also impossible to turn back the hands of time. That last moment is gone. And it's impossible to dislike someone who's trying to help you.

Think about that. You cannot help but like someone who is trying to help you. After all, it would make little sense to.

Knowing this, that people develop a true affection towards those who help them, don't you have the ability to be thought of fondly by others? You absolutely do. You can endear people to you by going out of your way to find ways to help them. Take action on this today!

-90-
Positive Outlook; Productive Results

There is no debate: Events and activities can be a great way to find and build wonderful professional relationships. So, be sure to work these into your schedule as often as your personal and professional life will allow.

While your mere presence is important to success, you will totally undermine your efforts if you bring with you anything but a positive disposition.

Now, not every day can be a good one, but chances are no day is a complete debacle. So, before you arrive do what you can to put forth an uplifting spirit. Listen to music. Have some coffee. Or both.

Remember, while support groups can be a networking opportunity, most networking events are not designed to be support groups. So, leave your worries at the door, to the extent possible. Show up with a positive outlook, a smile on your face and ready to meet people.

-91-
Be a Leader

Ever notice how most leaders have well developed networks? It is true. Leaders are well connected. The fact is that an advantage of any type of leadership position is that it gives you a built-in excuse for developing relationships. And with relationships, voilà, comes a network.

So, to build your network, take on some leadership.

Now, the thought of a leadership position might seem daunting because of the perceived required commitments. That's understandable. There is a way, however, to 'have your cake and eat it too.'

To do so, consider taking a more behind-the-scenes leadership role – such as chairing a committee or even assisting a main officer. This will serve to give you some of the same exposure of leadership without completely immersing you in the responsibility. And this gives you the opportunity for developing relationships and, voila, building a network.

-92-
The Apprehension Towards Small Talk

For many, the thought of engaging in "small talk" makes them anxious. This might be you.

This anxiety comes down to one simple thing - FEAR. Fear of being rejected. Fear of having nothing to contribute. Fear of getting stumped (or running out of conversation). Well, fear not!

First, you have things to contribute. You do! Your life is unique - a new and interesting story for someone else.

Second, you aren't going to be stumped. After all, much of the conversation will be about listening to the other person.

As for rejection, know this: Everyone is somewhat anxious about small talk. EVERYONE. Even the most well-connected, confident person will tell you that, deep down inside, they have this apprehension. So, if everyone feels this, then anyone will be relieved that you're talking with them.

So, go make someone's day. Engage in some "small talk."

-93-
Caring Equals Impact

Making a great impact is not about being the smartest person in the room. It's not about being impeccably dressed, either. Or having a winning smile, a firm handshake or a well-rehearsed personal introduction.

Making a great impact is best accomplished by simply demonstrating that others matter to you.

As Teddy Roosevelt is quoted as saying, "No one cares how much you know, until they know how much you care."

When you genuinely care about others, they'll become intrigued and want to know you. With this, they'll find they cannot help but like you. And while they won't be able to explain it, your presence will warm up their trust towards you.

When you care about others - genuinely care - you set in motion the mechanism that builds impactful relationships.

So, with this insight, continually ask yourself, "How can I demonstrate that others matter?"

-94-
Nametag Know-How

Nametags: That's a staple of most any networking event or gathering of professionals. And these three-inch, self-sticking billboards can be a real asset, if you follow these guidelines.

First, it's most important to show your first name, big and bold. Then legibly add in your last name and affiliation. Don't fuss with titles or other designations.

Also, as you write out your name tag, avoid scripts or cursive. That can be hard to read. Don't use icons or emojis. They can be confusing.

You're best to use only big, bold block letters in all caps or print using upper- and lower-case letters.

Finally, place your name tag on the right side, just below your collar bone, creating an easy sightline for the person reaching out to shake your hand.

These simple, but important, guidelines will serve you at any event.

-95-
The Cracked Pot

A woman had two large pots, each hung on the ends of a pole, which she carried across her neck. Daily, she walked to the stream, filled the pots, and took them home for chores.

One pot was perfect but the other had a crack in it, resulting in the cracked pot arriving only half full each day.

After years, the cracked pot spoke to the woman. "I am so ashamed. I leak all the way back home each day."

The woman simply smiled and said, "Did you notice that there are flowers on your side of the path? That's because, knowing about your flaw, I planted seeds there and you've been watering them. Why, without you, we would not have those beautiful flowers."

We all have our own unique imperfections. It is up to each of us to determine whether these shortcomings will be a liability or an asset.

-96-
Superbrat Loses Millions

John McEnroe was an icon in the world of tennis. He won hundreds of tennis matches and attained the No. 1 ranking in both singles and doubles, finishing his career with 77 singles and 78 doubles titles. He won seven Grand Slam singles titles, four at the US Open and three at Wimbledon, and added nine men's Grand Slam doubles titles. And he helped the U.S. win five Davis Cups.

Despite all these accomplishments, McEnroe is remembered as the "Superbrat" due to his outrageous outbursts and language towards tennis officials. While this behavior didn't hurt his tennis performance, it caused him to lose millions from advertising campaigns, product endorsements and sponsorship deals.

Remember this. Your performance may help you keep a job or maintain a business. But in the end, being nice will make you money. Talent is important, but not more important than character.

-97-
Improve on the Move

If you're listening to this, you are committed to your personal development and growth. Kudos.

Don't stop there, however. Think about how much time you spend commuting. Thirty minutes to work. Thirty minutes home. Maybe more. Multiply that by five days a week. Four weeks a month. Twelve months a year. Year after year.

Do the math. That time adds up. Why waste that time listening to debates over meaningless sports rankings? Why lose it to unseen talking heads taking outlandish political positions?

Rather devote your idle commute time to productive use. Use it to listen to programs that serve to educate, inspire, or motivate you. We live in a wonderful time. For mere pennies an hour or outright free, you have access to top notch podcasts and other audio programs.

So, pick a program, hit play and feel your knowledge grow.

-98-
Quick Tip on Small Talk

Small talk is important, know that. But here is the important thing about it. "Small talk" is not about filling idle time with interesting things to say. Rather, "small talk" is about getting the other person to fill time with things to say and you genuinely finding interest in them.

To make this happen, you need to be prepared with a small handful of open-end questions. Something like "Isn't this economy crazy?" will not cut it. However, something like "How does this economy affect your business?" just might.

Ask the question. Then, take an interest in what they have to say.

To show you've been listening summarize what you have heard. Then, just like the instruction on the shampoo bottle – lather, rinse, and repeat - ask another open-ended question.

By being interested in them, they will come to know, like and trust you.

-99-
The Time Between

It's important to remember that you should commit time to attending events and activities where you can interact with others in the business community. These might be … Prospective clients. Colleagues. Vendors. Even people in completely unrelated industries. This is important to establishing great new relationships and reconnecting with those you already know.

If you want more from your connections, however, look to the time between these interactions to "turbo charge" your relationships.

This is not to say that you must commit to spending hours and hours with these contacts. Simply stay engaged with them outside of events. You know, have a one-on-one over coffee, grab a bite to eat, play a round of golf, talk on the telephone, fire around e-mails. If you discipline yourself to this sort of engagement, you'll amplify what comes from your network.

-100-
Happiness Is a Choice

It probably comes as no surprise but given a choice, people would rather connect others to share information with, refer business to, and generally associate with happy people. Happy people have better and more productive relationships as a result.

Why is this? Simple. Happy people are just more fun to be around. Happy people are perceived to be easier to get along with. Happy people seem to be in control of their emotions and thus are more predictable to interact with.

None of this is a surprise, right? We are quick to come to know, like and trust happy people.

Knowing this, be happy. But here's the thing: Happiness depends solely on what you think. No life is not perfect, but in any moment, you and you alone get to choose whether or not you'll be happy. So, choose to be happy.

-101-
Stop Picking Up Any Old Rock

Gold miners didn't stuff their sacks with any old rocks. No, they were selective – choosing only those rocks where they perceived value. Makes sense, right?

Now, think of the activity of mining as a metaphor for working networking events. To effectively "mine" the event, you must focus on the value of each connection rather than on the quantity in the room.

In the long run, a few quality connections will benefit you more than a pocket full of business cards. Networking events are a useful means of connecting you with others who you can help and who can help you.

But here is the reality: Any gathering of people – a party, tradeshow, or after-hours event - can be a networking event. Mine these events wisely to expand the base of connections from which you build relationships. And then, in these relationships, you will find gold.

There you have it—101 essays. But we wanted to offer a bonus essay. Before we do, if you're interested in exploring other books, content, and programs by Frank Agin, visit frankagin.com or simply search "Frank Agin" on whatever platform you use to get great content.

Now here's your bonus essay.

-102-
The Law of Two Feet

Michael Roderick, host of *The Access to Anyone* Podcast, shared in his *Investing In People* newsletter the concept of the Law of Two Feet. He said, "Simply put the Law of Two Feet states that everyone has the right to walk away at any time."

In the newsletter he was referring to seminar activities and events, but the notion of The Law of Two Feet is much broader. In fact, you're up against every day relative to the people in your network. People can walk out of your life – literally and figuratively – at any point. They have that right.

But you can keep them tethered to you by subtlety providing an ongoing hope that you have value for them. It might be the prospects of introductions, or business opportunities. Or a sense that you're a source of strength and guidance when they need it most. Whatever the case, you have the power to keep their two feet firmly planted in your world.

About The Author

Frank Agin is president of AmSpirit Business Connections, which empowers entrepreneurs, sales representatives, and professionals to become successful and gain more referrals through networking.

He also shares information and insights on professional relationships, business networking and best practices for generating referrals on his Networking Rx podcast and through various professional programs.

Finally, Frank is the author of several books, including *Foundational Networking: Building Know, Like & Trust to Create a Life of Extraordinary Success*. See all his books and programs at frankagin.com. You can reach him at frankagin@amspirit.com.

www.ingramcontent.com/pod-product-compliance
Lightning Source LLC
Chambersburg PA
CBHW040757220326
41597CB00029BB/4970